Ann's Poems
of
Faith

Ann Linda Brenneman

Book Design, Typing and Editing By Norman E. Sindlinger

Dedication

To my family and friends and fellow believers in Jesus Christ.

Contents

Tonight

As day turns to night
I think of the angels flying
to us for our protection
through each and
every night.

Tonight, I pray that Christ
heals diseases by His word.
Fills the hungry and lifts the
poverty stricken up to a far
better life than before.

The night is short and at
times uneven for me.
Praise Jesus Christ.
Praise God.

At The Mass

I am finished with the crazy mass
Brethren meant to disdain women
at the mass. I'll watch for God, who
I hope still loves women. It is a
hard-won faith with all the bars to
God for women. Living Lutheran is
what I seek. A place to worship God
and Christ as a woman.

Not just to serve but to lead other
women to God and Christ. Pastor
Reverend Wendy opened me up to
church where women are recognized
by Christ and God. I will watch for
God to feed the hungry again tomorrow.
May the hungry use God's abundance
as the host and the clean water as the
blood for communion.

A full stomach and a clean cup of
drinking water is enough faith for these
men and a large gathering of women
and children.

Crazy mass has lots of
vestments, gold cups and plates, fancy
candles, printed hymns, choir, musicians,
and brethren. I will watch God's Almighty
Hand bend down to earth to feed His
poor congregation in Africa.

The Women

The weeping women stayed the night
after the rock was rolled away from the
tomb of their Lord, Jesus Christ.

The Roman bears also were there and
The women were fearful and afraid. The
bears looked up and so did the women.

They saw Jesus at a large table finishing
His Passover. His robes were white and He
was happy. "I am with my Father," said Jesus.

The women looked and saw two chairs at the
Passover table. "It is God and Jesus Christ," the
women said as they began to sing with forty bears.

The women and the bears went to Rome to see Caesar and tell him all the things Caesar didn't see, since they fell dead when God and Jesus arrived near a falling star in the sky.

Who Comes?

Who comes in the name of the Lord?
Who comes, who comes?
Who comes in the name of the Lord?
The sick, the old, the babe all
comes in the name of the Lord.

The Lord is good, the Lord is God.
They all came to the Lord of us all.
Who comes, who comes in His name?
Every day who comes in the name
of the Lord?

Praise God.
Praise Jesus Christ.

She Loves

Amazed of her grace
She loves
Convicted of her
Happiness

She loves
He, who has life is eternal
She loves
Country of her birth and service

She loves
Each and every day made by God
She loves
Strong and full of Jesus Christ

She loves
America, America
She loves
Praise God
Praise Jesus Christ

Truth

The truth is, wherever
and whenever you say
Jesus Christ is Lord.

Those who incline their
ear to the people will lead,
sayeth Lord Jesus Christ.

Those who incline their
ear to God will learn
Jesus Christ is Lord,
our savior and King.
Jesus Christ is Lord

Find A Way

To my wisdom; old and new
Kindness, respect, dignity
Glad, forgive, listen
Walk softly.

Power is immense
He believes in you
Be courageous
And be bold.

Hope will guide you
You'll find a way
Love deeply and
love truly.

Give freely from your heart
You'll surely know strife
But live your life
Blessed wonder
I believe.

Praise Jesus Christ
Praise God.

My Soul

What soul shall I give Jesus?
My soul, my soul; will it come back
renewed if I give my soul to Jesus?
How does it happen, the conversion
of souls?

Must I give to Him, or does He give to me?
My soul, it lacks what I need most—clarity,
steadfastness, confidence in my soul.
Jesus Christ has taught us this. Why do I
not have it for me?

Am I left behind Him? My soul, Christ
brought it to me from Him to me. My
Christian soul. Praise the Lord.

Jesus Christ.
Praise God.

When Jesus Weeps

When Jesus weeps in
the garden we all shall weep.
What rends his heart and burns
in His soul? It's our sin.
Our unrepented sin.
Jesus, our Savior, Lord, Protector,
Teacher and Friend has some
consolation from us, his
children, in grace and
love of God.
Should we continue to console
Jesus with God's graces and love
as children? Or do we now know
what weeping is to the son
of man, Jesus Christ?
Amen

The Big Rock

Have you ever sat on the
Big Rock Fountain for imagination?
Rock for physical exercise?
Stone for blood and water?

When John was little, he and
Grandma Martha made water
from that stone for blood
and water.

He became it. If it could do
this, it could do that. None
of the rest of us
remember,
but it.

Praise God. Praise the
Lord, Jesus Christ.

What Will Jesus Do Today?

Heal the sick.
Lead the flock.
Teach the novice.
Raise the dead who are in
their repose waiting for Him.

What will Jesus Christ do today?
Kiss you and send you out to the world
Stand next to you as you doubt.
Surprising people when He speaks.
Speak so all the world hears Him
and does His will.

What will Jesus Christ do today?
Comfort the bereft.
Treat us to His divine love.
He will go to our Father and intercede
again, to stop tyranny, unhappiness,
poverty and hunger.

Disease will flee at the word of Christ.
He will do this today.
Amen.

Mornings With Jesus

Have you seen Jesus Christ
giving His love to you?
Yes, I've seen Jesus Christ
at my church and my
whole life through.
Have you loved

Jesus Christ as He has
loved you? Is it possible to
love Him just as He loves you?
None of us can praise Christ
as much as he praises us.

Times of Christ

We don't live in times like these.
We live in times of Christ.
Jesus lives to protect those who
hear Him clearly, and do His and
our Almighty Father's will.

We don't live in times of hunger.
We live in times of Christ.
Jesus lives to show us the
abundance of our Father Almighty.
We don't live in times of civil strife.
We live in times of Christ.

Jesus lives to have the government
on His shoulders

Next Year

He too is in next year.
Everyday thousands that year
make the decision whether to trust God.

It's just to access each day.
It has taken most of these
to transform last year.

It required a steadfast belief,
and there was God.
He wrote in real time.

Before long, more than his day.
Rewarded for a year to grow
almost effortlessly were changing
and had to try to calm this long
We would end up each other.

I really respond.
Early insight.
Was to link people.
Praise God.

I Am

I am, I am, I am.
I am, I am, I am.

We live in times of Christ.
We will praise God.
Take two steps now.

Step in God's footprints.
I am, I am, I am.
We don't live in times like these.

We live in times of Christ.
We will have praise God.
Praise God.
Praise God.

Prayer

Pray for the Holy Father, Praise God.
Praise Jesus Christ. Has there ever been
a more beautiful prayer other than the
Lord's Prayer?

This prayer supersedes the Law and
The Papal Father. Let the Canon Law
respond as presented to us by the
Holy Father.

Let the Canon Law respond to the
heart of all Christians and other
Faiths. The Law is changing but not
God's love and Christ Jesus' sacrifice.

Black Lives Matter

Matter.
Matter of Soul.
Matter of Holy Spirit.
Matter of sins.

Matter of prayer.
Matter of Christ Jesus.
Matter of God.

Black lives matter.
All God's ministries matter.
All God's clay, wood, water,
and flesh. Matter is calm.
Matter explodes.

Matter of Earth.
Matter of outer space.
Praise God, Praise.
Jesus Christ, Holy Spirit.

Praise God.
This is a living Lutheran.

God's World

The world's major diseases are a
mere breath away from God's cures.
Some remain still secret yet a cure
for everyone is consecrated in our
Lady of Fatima's sacred heart.

For God so loved the world that he
gave the life of his only begotten son
so that we may all have life, and have
it abundantly with God's bright word
in each cell of our bodies.

Please feed the world's hungry
With God's word in each bowl.

Praise God

All is for thanksgiving to God
All is for the joy of Christ Jesus
Never is for the Virgin Mary
Forever and ever is for the
espoused Joseph, earthly
father to the Son of God.

A man is for God's eternal
love for His creation
Praise the Holy Spirit
Praise Jesus Christ
Praise for Alleluia
Praise God.

Christ Is Triumphant

Christ is triumphant over death
Through the Holy Eucharist, we
can be and are triumphant over
sexual abuse and violence
against God's creation.
The word of God.

God is in each empty food
bowl, so it will always be full.
We can overcome world hunger,
end the scourge of cancer, and
be released to space travel.

God is merciful in His healing.
The empty cross, the empty tomb.
The risen Christ.
Our Savior.

Our Redeemer.

Peace City

Civil disobedience—yes. Yet, most people still remain on the side of peace. We have a budget for peace. Peace city—the assembly at Chautauqua Institution, New York taught me how.

Many people really love, create and live peace. FDR gave his famous presidential speech, "I hate War" at the Amphitheatre. The peace budget is a trillion dollars per year.

"I will underwrite it if it is kicked to the curb by our elected representatives. The Peace Bill will be presented by the elected, appointed or anointed person with the least Experience in the public eye/media."

Peace City.
Amen

Christ Is Risen

Alleluia, Christ is risen.
Today is unlike other days
because we say Alleluia
Christ is risen.

The stars talk to people
Especially stars of
show business.

God has dealt with Satan
completely. I renounce
Satan and all his evil
deeds.

I pray to our Risen Christ
and our Father Almighty.
Praise God.

Joyful

Joyful, joyful we adore thee
Son of man and son of God
Joyful thanks to thee.

My savior is my Lord Jesus Christ
My God is the Father Almighty
Maker of heaven and earth

I live the redemption and resurrection
Of my Lord Jesus Christ
Praise God

Praise Jesus Christ
Praise the Holy Spirit
Jesus is with me
God is with me

Praise God

We love. Praise God
We love. Praise Jesus Christ.
We have. Praise Holy Spirit.
We have. Amen.

We have. Alleluia.
We have the Lord's Prayer
We have the Apostle's Creed.
We have the Nicene Creed.
We have the Risen Christ.

We have the Bride of Christ.
The empty cross because
we live the Risen Christ.
The empty cross continues
to change everything.

Only Son

Your only Son,
Jesus Christ
Went to his passion
through His Faith.
The Lord, our God
passed Christ His cup.

Christ drank from it.
It was bitter some say
with His tears for all
those so much in need.

Peace, love, righteousness,
forgiveness, hope, charity, mercy
He brought to the world.

Alleluia.
Amen.

My Prayer

Feed the Hungry.
Quench their thirst.
House the homeless.
Clothe the naked.
Heal the sick.

Give hope to all those
who have none.
Gather all without faith.
Teach them to love.

Show them forgiveness.
Hear my prayer, Lord.
Have mercy on us, Lord.
End conflict. Bring peace.

God In My Life

I feel God in my life
like I never have before.
It is the most remarkable
change for my heart.

I loved things in the world,
not of God. God bless Christ
Jesus and all the saints today
On All Saints Day.

God Almighty is my eternal
father teaching me God's way
not humankind's way.

God, Jesus Christ, and the Holy
Spirit are all I really wanted and
Needed in my spiritual life.
Amen.

I Praise God

I praise God because He brings love.
My Father Almighty is the author of my faith. I
worship my Father Almighty as I do His son. I
renounce Satan and all of his devious works.

I know God continues to deal with Satan's
evil schemes and continues to confine him
in a black hole in space, most have no way out.
Unfortunately, evil's power is hard to contain.

Evil hides in places mostly untouchable by us.
God's love and power reach out to guard our
hearts and souls. With God's love and protection,
we are safe with our Lord Jesus Christ.

Amen.
Praise God.
Praise our Lord

Rap Star

David, you are a rap star, rap star
David, you are a rap, rap star.

David, you are blue.
David, you are blue.
David, you are a blue
rap star.

Blue rap star, rock star.
Blue rap star, rock star.
David, you are a blue rap star, rock star.
Blue star. Blue star. David.

David, a blue star.
Rap star, rock star.

Dear Holy Father

I am Lutheran, Pro-Life, and a 65 year
old, disabled woman who wants to study
Canon law through prayer.

Can you recommend a laser path for me
so I can be part of the church in Rome,
and my home church in Pompton Plains, NJ?

Sincerely in Christ,
Ann Linda Brenneman

Our Father

Praise to my Father Almighty, my love
taught to me by Jesus Christ, praise
my love to God. I renounce Satan and
all his works and deeds. God has dealt
with Satan. I do not energize my enemies
since my strength is from my Father
Almighty Christ Jesus and the Holy Spirit.

 I am not going to waste words with
anything less than Praise to God,
Love to God. Obedience to God's
love is my greatest grace today. Each
grace is added unto me. Praise God,
Praise I am, I am. Praise to Mary mother
of God. Praise to Jesus Christ who taught
me to pray.

Our Father who art in heaven hallowed be
thy name. Thy kingdom come, thy will be
done, on earth as it is in heaven.

God's Kingdom

We will have Praise God.
Watch your data entry.
Use your prayer skills.
We will have Praise God.

Praise God.
Praise Jesus Christ.
Praise Mary, mother of God.
Praise God.

Unending kingdom of God
Praise God.
Praise Jesus Christ.
Praise Jesus Christ.

Praise God.
World without end.
An A-men Kingdom. Praise God.
Praise God.

Praise God that I see your mighty hand
feed the hungry with their empty bowls.
This morning, I will pray your name, God.
God forever and ever amen.

Praise God for those with no hands or arms.
Praise God for those unable to feed themselves.
I pray for all who live in your blessed kingdom.
God, I pray you'll heal all the sick and the lame.

With God

The talk and walk of God.
That is the talk and walk we need now.
Pro-Life includes saving the lives of our
armed forces. God bless them and keep
them safe.

The maternity home is a coast to coast
reality. Bless the mother who is a
Homemaker with enough money. Bless
the women homemakers who also work
outside their home and have a living wage.

Lord, strengthen me to sign New Jersey's
law for tuition free community colleges and
trade schools. Lord, let John Jay Criminal
Law College in NYC be tuition free. Lord, let
me be strong enough to attend the Tuesday
meeting.

I renounce Satan. God has dealt with him and placed him in a black hole in space with no way in and no way out. Let me use prayer so that all people and all creatures great and small renounce Satan entirely. Lord, let us see your bright word when we look to You and our Lord Jesus Christ.

The Will of the People

Did our Congressional Representatives
and Senators forget why they are there?
The will of the people. Is it the law in a
democracy to follow the will of the people?

Our leaders represent us, yet it is the will of
the people to judge them. The law is stone
unless it is written from the heart. Our new
covenant was brought to us through The
Crucifixion of God's only son, Jesus Christ
our savior and our Lord.

Flags Among the Flowers

Flags among the flowers is our blessed nation. Charity to all. Liberty and justice for all. Come, let us live as humble Americans under God, with the pledge of allegiance to the flag of The United States of America, and to the republic for which it stands, one nation under God with liberty and justice for all.

Flags among the flowers. Our country has ample stores of grain. Our country has flowers in the White House gardens. Especially famous is the Rose Garden that blooms for the President.

Praise God.
This is living Lutheran Ann.

I Believe In God

I believe in God our Father Almighty.
Creator of heaven and earth.
I believe in Jesus Christ, His only son,
our Lord, who was conceived by the
Holy Spirit, born of the Virgin Mary,
suffered under Pontius Pilot, was
crucified, died, and was buried on the
third day.

He rose from the dead, ascended into
Heaven and is seated at the right hand
of God, the Father Almighty. From here
He shall come again to judge the living
and the dead.

I believe in the Holy Catholic and apostolic
Church, the communion of spirits, the
forgiveness of sins, the resurrection of the
body, and the everlasting.
Amen.
Praise God.

Happiness

Happiness is a good soul, dedicated to God and to His son, Jesus Christ. I notice the change in my happiness when I take communion once a week. Now, I can feel my happiness grows as the goodness of God and Christ continue to increase.

This is the abundance, full, tamped down, secreted in my soul when I take communion. Glorious Lord Jesus, Ruler of all nations, son of God, son of man. Beautiful Savior, Lord of the earth, sun, moon, stars, and sky. My happiness is without end. I am full of joy.

Sanctuary

Lord, may Your church sanctuary be truly
available to those victims of poverty, strife,
war, and abortion. Set them free of their
pain at Your altar and have communion with
them.

Let your speeches to these people inspire
them in faith to Mary, Jesus, and Joseph.
Let them believe in Christ so that these
people are ready for Your peace and Your
redemption. Let the Holy Spirit be with
them to withstand the rigorous life they
live.

Help our people who do their best to live
under their burden of poverty. Lord God.
Let me find a way to find enough money
to help those I can.

Our Father, who art in heaven, hallowed
be thy name. Thy Kingdom come, thy will
be done, on earth as it is in heaven. Give
us this day our daily bread, and forgive us
our trespasses as we forgive those who
trespass against us. Lead us not into
temptation but deliver us from evil, for thine is the
Kingdom and the power and the glory forever and
ever.
Amen

I Love God

In my heart, I love God.
In my heart, I love the Holy Family.
Jesus Christ, Virgin Mary, and Joseph.
The "I love you" goes to the face I see
on other people. God is with them. God
makes these people's faces glow with joy.

How can I not praise God and Jesus Christ?
No ifs, and's or buts. No what, when, and
where. The Holy Spirit is our comforter
on earth and in heaven.

I love God.
I love God.
I love God.

The Abandoned Cross

It was dark at the abandoned cross and the
women of the cross were frantic at where
their Lord's body and clothing remnant had
gone. He was taken away, but they only had
a tomb to look into. They looked and saw
their Lord in brilliant, white robes.

"Do not touch me for I have not yet ascended
to my Father." The women wept after He
appeared; they stopped after He spoke to them.
The other crosses still held bodies hanging
terribly. At the site, the Roman soldiers took the
bodies down and left them in an open grave.

Some made jewelry with the crucified Christ
clinging in death for them on the cross. Others,
more hopefully I think, have the abandoned
cross of the risen Christ. Their messiah, gone
to His Father in heaven.

Endnote

Thank you for reading my book *Poems of Faith*. I hope that you enjoyed my poems as much as I did writing them.

If you enjoyed my poems, I'd very much appreciate your taking a few minutes of your valuable time to leave a review on Amazon.